growing up
an alien

aoife mannix

tall-lighthouse

*This book is dedicated to
my parents, Joan and Tony*

Growing up an Alien was first presented in two scratch
performances for the Southbank Centre's London Literature
Festival on July 11 2007. A full version was first performed
at the Cotton Gallery, mac, Birmingham on October 12 2007.

Written and performed by Aoife Mannix

Music written and performed by Janie Armour

Design by Kerry Bradley

Directed and produced by Mike Kirchner for Apples & Snakes

With extra special thanks to Sarah Ellis

Some of these poems, or versions of these poems, first
appeared in Citizen 32, Aesthetica, and Wow! Magazine.

With many thanks for all their help, inspiration and
encouragement - Zak Akhimien, Janie Armour, Arts
Council England, Apples & Snakes, Jacky Arnold, Battersea
Arts Centre, Charles Beckett, Malika Booker, Kerry Bradley,
Central Foundation School for Girls, Geraldine Collinge,
Martin Colthorpe, Rosa Conrad, Sandra Davenport,
Louisa Davies, Charlotte Dove, Jenny Doyle, Zena Edwards,
Nick Field, John G Hall, Mark Hewitt, Mike Kirchner, Lit Up,
mac, Malika's Poetry Kitchen, Eamonn Mannix, Stephen
Mannix, Deirdre McCarthy, Lisa Mead, Kate Morgenroth,
Joan O'Connell, Oily Cart, Our Lady's Hospice Harold's
Cross, Roger Robinson, St Paul's Catholic School,
Sarah Sanders, Southbank Centre, Siw Thomas,
Christine Walters, Naomi Woddis

Cover photo Andy Rumball

APPLES & SNAKES

ARTS COUNCIL ENGLAND

ISBN 978-1-904551-39-3
tall-lighthouse
www.tall-lighthouse.co.uk

contents

introduction

biographies

introduction

Growing up an Alien started out as one poem
that I gradually enlarged to become over two hours
worth of material. This then had to be edited back to
make a one hour performance. The first line of the
original poem was 'born in Stockholm in a snow storm on
the stroke of midnight' and in a way everything I've
written for the show relates back to this first image. I
wanted all the poems, whether funny or sad, to keep a
certain sense of childish wonder and discovery. Images
of snow and ice recur in quite a few of the poems. For
me, they represent the beauty and dangers of exploring
alien environments and thus how I felt growing up.

I first discussed the idea of doing a theatrical
poetry and music show with Geraldine Collinge, director
of Apples & Snakes, England's leading organisation for
performance poetry. Although much of my writing is
quite autobiographical and personal, I had never before
attempted to link my poems in a sequence that would
partially tell my life story. This represented quite a
challenge but also an opportunity to really examine what
I was trying to say. Arts Council England supported an
initial period of research and development for the show
in the summer of 2006. As part of this, I ran creative
writing workshops and interviewed students in a boys'
school and a girls' school about their experiences
of growing up in London. The intelligence and
insightfulness of their responses allowed me to look at
my own experiences in new ways. In particular, the fear
of violence and intimidation that many of the boys spoke
of made me think about expectations of masculinity and
what my own brothers had been through. Many of the
girls I worked with were from a British Asian
background. Their understanding of the gap between
themselves and their mothers, the conflict, respect and
deep love that they felt, helped me to look at my own
relationship with my mother.

I then spent a week in a rehearsal studio with
producer Mike Kirchner work shopping ideas for how the
show could develop. I've always been fascinated by the
idea of exploring how poetry and music can work
together. I think poetry lies somewhere between prose
and music in that the rhythm and the sound are as
important as the meaning of the words. We asked a
number of musicians, including Janie Armour, to respond
to what I'd written so far.

At the end of the week, we presented about 30 minutes worth of material to a small invited audience. In September 2006, myself and Janie performed a ten minute extract from the show at Lit Up, a showcase for arts professionals at the Brewery Arts Centre in Kendal.

This was followed by script meetings between myself and Mike. I wrote each part as an individual poem, but Mike helped me to look at the structure of the overall piece, to see what was missing, to rewrite what didn't quite work, and to cut what wasn't necessary. In June I spent three days with Mike, Janie, and designer Kerry Bradley preparing for two scratch performances at the Southbank Centre. We presented a 45 minute extract followed by a post show discussion with the audience. Though I was nervous at the idea of discussing work in progress in a public forum, I actually found it a really useful experience. Audience members had so much enthusiasm for and interesting ideas about how the show could develop, especially with regards to how the different elements of poetry, music, performance and design could be made to compliment each other that I entered the three week rehearsal process with a great feeling of excitement.

The idea of having this book, which serves as both a programme for the show and a small poetry collection, came about through discussions with Les Robinson, director of tall-lighthouse, who edited and published my previous collection *the elephant in the corner*. Our aim is to demonstrate that poetry can be appreciated both in performance and on the page and to try to expand the boundaries of what poetry is expected to be.

I hope you enjoy it.

Aoife Mannix
October 2007

Prologue

The smell of a tangerine peeled
in the depths of a forest covered in snow,
the purity of that orange freshness
when you strip away the layers of skin.

Underneath all the unnecessary noise,
there is a silence so magic it wraps me
in a soft cocoon of whiteness.

A snowflake melting on my tongue.

This moment when I rest
under the heaviness of the trees,
stare out at the mountains
scraping against a sky so blue it hurts.

The air itself is crystal truth.

I sit in the quiet of this alien landscape,
a small space explorer, a snow
cosmonaut landed from Mars.

And all around me there is nothing but wonder.

Making Tea

We are the only light left on in the hospice, a single glowing window suspended amongst the ghosts of closed eyes. As if the rest of the world had vanished and there is only this room, this night left. I look out at the stars I no longer remember the names of, their animal shapes smudged since I lost my telescope. You always claimed I had a kaleidoscope smile but now there's nothing but glass in my mouth, the colours cut my tongue as we breathe this silence and I offer beverages as a last resort. You say, 'funny how much I thought I needed but now I'd give my right arm just to be at home drinking a decent cup of tea. Such a small thing to ask really when you think about it.' I reply, 'There's a kitchen just down the hall. I won't be long.' 'Take your time. I'm not going anywhere,' which we both know isn't true.

The kitchen is more of a cubicle but I find it easily because of the strip of fluorescent white gleaming under the door. I knock and a woman about your age opens it. It's 4am and I'm grateful not to be the only one brewing at this God forsaken hour. She says, 'the kettle's just boiled,' as if she's been expecting me. Then with a hint of defiance, 'I brought my own. I don't think it tastes the same from those metallic ones. Do you?' For a second the taste of tin rises up in my throat but I swallow it down. 'Why are you here?' she asks. 'My mother.' She nods and says, 'My sister.' And then because there is nothing else we need to say, she pours a drop of water into a blue teapot with white daisies on it, swirls this ocean, empties it, pops in two tea bags and fills it to the brim with infinite care. I watch this ritual as if seeing it for the very first time. 'It's gotten awful cold,' she smiles at me, 'I think it might snow you know.'

And suddenly I am spinning inside a snowflake, a million billion crystals are melting on my tongue, their patterns unique and unreadable. And I am falling, falling forever through infinite space, leaving the tiniest of footprints on the Milky Way. By morning, we'll be long gone.

Conception

My mother was married in Dublin in 1971
in a dress that nearly asphyxiated her
because God forbid I should be more
than a piece of star in my father's eye.

She used to sleep at alternate ends of the bed
to relieve the stultifying boredom
and dreamt of meeting a man
who could read passports.

Despairing of love, my father decided
to chance one last dance,
all he saw was the fire of her long red hair
and when my mother turned round
he thought, but she's just a child.

The song was Je t'aime,
they spoke to each other in French
and my mother thought
she probably wouldn't see him again.

She had plans to climb the Berlin Wall,
but he drove her around for a week whispering
'freedom is making a choice' till she agreed
he was her only hope of a visa.

So she ran away to be his idea of perfect,
to a fairy tale city coated in snow,
where they spent their mornings
in a storm of pillow fights
practising their Swedish
and renting porn films
that were banned back home.

My father joked he wasn't
that into spectator sports
so they had a baby instead.

Born in Stockholm in a snow storm
on the stroke of midnight,
the first thing I do is put my thumb in my mouth,
the nurse says it's a sign of intelligence,

then again this is the same nurse
who can't pronounce my name
so christens me Fifi.

My mother doesn't recognize me,
no one has warned her babies arrive
covered in goo and blood.

She thinks I'm an alien, a feeling she never manages
to shake off as she turns herself inside out
to keep me amused.

My parents raced me through the streets
of Stockholm in a green pram, their breath steaming
with laughter 'til they hit a bump in the path
and I sailed clean out into the snow.

For a second my mother's heart went completely still
as my father dashed to rescue me from the ice.

But I lay soft and unblinking, my eyes blue flakes,
and I never even cried as they put me back,
suddenly sober with the responsibility of flight.

Birth of a Younger Brother

April Fool's Day, 1975. I'm three years old
and I'm in my grandparents' house in Dublin
when I first meet my brother Stephen.
To be honest it's something of an anticlimax.
All that fussing and rushing around and me
having to stay with Nana and Granddad,
which admittedly isn't that bad 'cos though
it smells a bit funny, I get to colour in
the back of Christmas cards and wind
up the Spanish dancer twirling forever
on her wooden boat with the same tune
playing over and over. Besides they let me
eat far more biscuits than I get to at home.

Still it doesn't seem quite right,
my mother in the hospital, which is after all
where sick people go, though my Dad says
she isn't sick and a brother or a sister
will be a great playmate for me.

This is the cause of my disappointment
as I stare down into the Moses basket
because in fact my brother turns out to be
pink and considerably smaller than me,
and therefore not any use for playing with.
He doesn't even look like a doll 'cos dolls
don't scream so much or go bright red
when you pinch them. Plus there's something
wrong with his lungs so the doctor says,
if he wasn't being breast fed, he'd be dead.

I guess that's why he's always eating.

Gifts

I tell my Gran, 'my Daddy isn't really a prince, he just looks like one.' Like in Sleeping Beauty, we spend a lot of time waiting for him to turn up. This is because his job is to go round the world persuading all the bad guys to hand over their weapons. It's very important work but my mother says she's tired of playing Lois Lane and at least Clark Kent came home for his dinner.

I do my best to make the most of when he's around. Asking one evening in an effort not to have to go to bed, 'Daddy, guess what I did today? I went all the way to the end of the garden.' My father gasps in horror. 'You should never do that.' 'Why not?' 'There's trolls live down there. They eat little girls alive.' My mother says, 'stop trying to frighten her.' Which only convinces me further that the world is far more dangerous than I realise and I make up my mind never to venture to the end of the garden again.

But my Dad's not scared, he travels everywhere. He tells me how the magic lady in New York stole his tickles. Ignoring the filthy look my mother gives him, he shows me his passport covered in multicoloured stamps from mysterious places that exist behind a curtain made of iron. I'm fascinated by this book I can't read and never tire of his tales of two headed monsters, Kubla Khan, Russian spies, court intrigues. He brings back gifts of dolls that fit inside each other, wonderful puppets, magic jumping beans, a box that can make coins vanish. I can't help wishing he wasn't quite so good at disappearing tricks.

Origins

I start to contemplate my own future,
proudly announcing, 'when I grow up,
I want to be a hooker. You know, like Nana.'

My Dad is unimpressed
with this description of his mother,
'What are you talking about?'

'When she does the thing with the hooks,
you know, the needles.'

My mother laughs, 'That's crochet.'

But my Dad instead teaches me to say,
'when I grow up I want to be a nuclear physicist.'

I tell my brother, 'I'm Jason,
intergalactic warrior spy,
guardian of the universe,
we're not actually related.'

He says, 'I know, I was born in Dublin
but you were made in Sweden.'

Moving to Canada

I'm five years old and I'm sitting
at our kitchen table making a joke out of glass.

The red blue tiles slide
into each other with a kind of grace I love.

But I'm not thinking of this,
I'm not thinking of anything,

I'm listening to my parents
slot words into each other's mouths.

My father says, 'the second largest nation
on earth after the Soviet Union.'

I try to remember what his atlas looks like,
the countries stretched pink and raw.

I see myself in a jungle with monkeys
scrambling up palm trees.

Then my mother says,
'there's sure to be too much snow.'

So I wipe away this picture,
try to pretend the tiles are windows

I can see through;
there are suitcases in the air again.

Sailing

I'm running down a long corridor
searching for my name.

A O I F E, the vowels echo in my head,
but the wall is blank as the teacher explains
she didn't bother because I'm leaving so soon.
All the other kids have theirs but I've vanished,
already gone, even though I'm still here.

Like time travel as I comb my Nana's hair
and tell her I hope her and Granddad
won't die before I get back.

She says she'll pray for that.
Something in her face makes me realise
I don't actually know what death is.

Me and Granddad set up deck chairs in the garage,
one behind the other, and play indoor fishing.
I tell him there's a huge storm, giant waves
are crashing over the side of our ship
as I wave my rod around wildly.

He relights his pipe.

'There may be a storm in your part of the boat,
but in mine, it is the most peaceful sunny day.'

Time Difference

I'm looking through an aeroplane window
at hundreds of toy cars
laid out carefully below us.

My Dad claims they're not toys,
they're real, just very far away.
But I'm learning not to believe everything he says.

I'm walking through a fruit market,
there are piles of oranges and bananas and apples
all neatly arranged.

Suddenly I know my parents have been turned
into pieces of fruit and I'll never find them again.
I wake up silently screaming.

My mother says I'm overtired,
go back to bed. My Dad says it's jet lag,
which is something to do with clocks moving forward.

How it feels like day
even though it's night, how the past
catches up with the future.

Alike

We live in a hotel
because no one in Canada
moves house when it's snowing.
It snows for three months.

One day, my brother, aged three,
picks up a large glass ashtray
and hurls it at the wall.
It shatters into a thousand pieces.

My mother looks as if she's
about to shatter too. She asks
me to get the wooden spoon.
My brother stares at me unrepentant.

I run and fetch a dustpan and broom,
fall to my knees and start sweeping glass.
'Don't,' my mother yells.
'You'll cut yourself.'

Cleaning up every last shard
distracts her from the beating
my brother is due. The blizzard
of her anger passes into crystal blue skies

and she's smiling again.
'It's okay,' she tells him.
'Sometimes I feel like
smashing things too.'

Learning to Skate

On the Rideau Canal in Ottawa,
a young girl is being taught how to skate
by her father. It's bitter cold
on the frozen water, her breath
cracking in clouds of confusion,
her cheeks blue flames.

She struggles to find a balance,
but her skates keep slipping.
Losing patience, her father tells her
to stay put 'til he returns.

She sits in a bank of snow
with the chill settling into her bones,
a certain childish stubbornness
sliding down her spine.

She struggles to her feet,
places the edge of the blade
on to the curve of ice, and suddenly
she's gliding, as if she's found the rhythm
of a secret dance, a magic elegance.

Other skaters slice past
in a swirl of coats and scarves,
such speed and grace. She stops suddenly,
a strange sense of freedom
sweeping up inside her,
the crest of a wave about to break.

She wants to show her father she can do it at last.

But he's nowhere in sight.
And there's only a vast whiteness
that has swallowed up the space
where she was supposed to wait.

She feels then the thinness of the ice,
its treacherous mirrors, scarred promises,
and a fear that turns her feet to stone.

Girls

It's summertime in World War II
and the Nazis have invaded our sandpit.
I'm brandishing a small red plastic water pistol.
Admittedly not nearly as cool as my father's rifle
which I've had to lend to Philip, my best friend
Blare's evil older brother who tells me
every time he sees me, 'I hate girls.
Girls are sissies. They stink.'
I imagine taking a revolver like 007 has
and putting it to Philip's head and the look
of surprise on his face just before I blow his brains out.

Picking a moment when the Nazis are looking
the other way, I sprint across the lawn and take up
a new position behind the hedge. I beckon for Blare
to follow me. He hesitates, then makes a dash for it,
unfortunately tripping over his own shoelace
and landing with a cry of pain.

The Nazis are instantly upon us.
They drag us before their leader Philip,
who today bears an even closer resemblance
to Adolf Hitler than usual. He flings my father's rifle
at my feet. 'That piece of shit doesn't work anymore.'
I can see the wood's splintered, he's broken the catch
right off. My Dad's going to kill me. Blare starts
to cry, which is what I feel like doing
but I'd never give them the satisfaction.

'See that's what happens when you play with girls,'
Philip roars at his little brother. 'You're to quit
doing it. Tell her, go on, tell her.' I look at Blare,
pleading not to be betrayed. But he's staring
at his feet. 'You're not my friend any more.'
Philip laughs, shoving me so hard
I fall backwards into the sand, then marches
away with Blare as his captive.

I know it's not my friend's fault I'm a girl,
but I'm still heart broken.

In Irish

We move back from Canada to the suburbs of Dublin.
An bhfuil cead agam dul amach go dti an leatheroid
mas e thoil e doesn't exactly roll off the tongue when
you're seven years old. But this is what my teacher
pronounces I need to say when nature calls.
The literal translation being, 'can I go outside to the
toilet please?' My bladder nearly bursts as I struggle
to master my grandfather's native tongue.

We're learning the story of St Patrick. I raise my hand
and ask how the whole thing works, father, son, holy
ghost, same being. My teacher says it's a miracle.
'But how do they actually do it, three in one, how's
it possible?' I genuinely want to know but my teacher's
annoyed and makes me stand with my face
against the blackboard.

My new best friend Grainne refuses to speak to me
because her father says we're the devil's children
because we don't go to mass. My Dad says neither
God nor fairies exist, there is no heaven or hell, no
garden of Eden, no Never Never Land. They're just
stories not worth getting out of bed on a Sunday for.
I try telling Grainne fairies aren't real. But she starts
to cry claiming I've killed one just by saying that so
I avoid any discussion of Jesus.

Being left without a God of my own, I decide to take
up sun worship like the Incas, though I reckon I won't
bother with the human sacrifice bit. I find a box in the
bathroom full of wonderful miniature cardboard
telescopes and practice staring at the sun till my eyes
water. My mother says these telescopes are private
tampons and I'm to leave them alone. Which seems
a bit mean 'cos she's got loads of them.

I remain determined to practice my own religion in
secret. Though I'm not sure it'll save me from eternal
damnation or Captain Hook's clock stopping or nuclear
war. I wish I shared my father's certainty of which
stories are true and which are not.

Heights

It's New Year, 1979, at Funderland in the RDS in
Dublin. In the cold calculation of the January air,
a young girl tries to talk her father into coming
on the roller coaster with her. It isn't that she's
mocking his fear, far from it, the reason she asks
is for the sheer thrill of hearing the story of why
her father is so utterly petrified of heights.
He closes his eyes and goes that little bit paler
just at the thought of it. She asks, 'What happened,
Dad?' 'I don't like to talk about it.'
'But what happened, Dad?'

Well it was several hundred years ago, back when
he was a small boy, and his father, her grandfather,
took him to Funderland, which was a lot smaller
then with no bumper cars. But there was this one
huge monstrosity of a spider with eight legs and
at the end of each leg there was a kind of bucket
where they strapped you in. Then the spider would
swish his legs at a faster and faster speed and the
buckets would toss and turn and spin you
completely upside down, but it was just about okay
because of the straps. But this one time, just as her
father and her grandfather were hanging upside
down at the highest possible point, the spider gave
a terrible groan and froze. The entire machine
shuddered to a complete stop, and her father
was trapped, suspended upside down for several
eternities while somebody ran to get an engineer.

Her father swears he can still hear that spider
breathing and how the world was completely
inverted until they got a ladder and helped him
down. He says, 'I know you must think I'm an awful
coward.' She reassures him, 'No, Dad, if that
happened to me I wouldn't want to get on
a roller coaster either.' And it's good to know
he has at least one fear he's prepared to admit to.

Grapes

We go to see my Granddad
in the hospital. He's a funny yellow colour
but he winks at me and offers me grapes.
I eat the whole bunch.

My Nana tells me
about a deer in the forest who got sick
and all the other animals who came to visit him
ate the deer's food and the deer starved to death.

My Granddad has a whistle
and when he blows it, it doesn't make a sound
but a robin red breast comes
and lands on the palm of his hand.
I wonder if the robin will visit him in hospital.

I run in from playing one evening
and my mother tells me my Granddad has died.
I laugh because I'm sure she's joking.

She's not, so I dash back into the street
to tell all my friends because that's what
the woman in Ali Baba and the Forty Thieves
does when she thinks Ali Baba's dead, she runs
from house to house wailing to the neighbours.

I wonder if my Granddad's really hidden
in a cave somewhere
where the walls are studded
with thousands of rubies and diamonds
and there's a magic genie. He'd like that.

I wish I hadn't eaten all his grapes.

The Madhatters

I'm eight years old and we move back from the
suburbs of Dublin to Dolphin's Barn, the inner city.
Next door live three old ladies. They're sisters, well
into their eighties, but to us kids, they seem beyond
time. They like to ask me and my brother in for cakes
on winter evenings. They have no electricity so their
front room remains lost in the romance of
candlelight. There are stacks of newspapers,
magazines everywhere. Their faded yellow prints
paw at us as we stand in the semi darkness breathing
the rustle of ancient books, the faint whiff of ghosts.
The eldest sister Sara is confined to a wheelchair.
She spends her days sitting in the window feeding
the budgies she keeps in an enormous cage. We love
those birds, their greens and sudden darts of yellow.
She tells us tales of their adventures in Africa with
such animation, we're all transported there.

And as we eat the strange sweet squares of pink icing
and sip our orange squash, they promise us this is
nothing. That one day we'll have a proper tea party,
just like Alice in Wonderland, with hats and
everything, and there'll be magic teapots that can
talk, and a cat that never stops smiling, and the
budgies will don their tuxedos, and they'll wear their
ball gowns, and my brother can sport his cowboy suit
if he wants. And we'll have an enormous birthday
cake shaped like an aeroplane that will zoom around
the room, and endless cups of tea that can refill
themselves.

When we leave, my brother whispers to me,
'do you think they really are witches?' I reply,
'It's hard to tell, we'll have to wait till we get the invite.'

Wish

Me and my best friend Deirdre
are holding dandelion clocks and wishing.

We fill our lungs and blow
as hard as ever we possibly can.

The seeds cling for a second,
then scatter into hundreds of wisps

of helicopters whirring in the breeze,
not a single one left standing on either stem.

'We did it.' Deirdre hugs me in delight.

I'm still clutching the empty stalk, a clock
now empty of numbers, a tiny moment of eternity.

I'm not sure I share her faith in magic
but nine months later there he is,

my baby brother Eamonn,
the most perfect wonderful miracle,

my wish come true.

Nursery Rhyme

My Dad teaches me,
Twinkle twinkle little star,
I know damn well what you are.
Circling up above so high,
super nova, super spy.
CIA and KGB,
stay away from little me.

Play with Me

Your bedroom was Russia,
and you built your armies from plastic monsters
and supersonic laser guns, but it was no use
because I was older and constructed an imaginary
force field to surround America as we conducted
our own Cold War, marrying off the princess
our Gran had given me to one of your gargoyles
in some strange ceremony of alliance
that lasted the whole afternoon
with the rain firing missiles against the window,
and you agreeing to the terms of my treaty
because you didn't know any better, and besides,
there was always the danger I'd declare the game
silly, and go off and read a book instead.

Because I could be like that sometimes, dead boring,
and superior, and on the edge of vanishing
into the world of hormones, boys and phone calls
that lasted for days. But for now the empire
had yet to crumble, so we mixed Star Wars
and spying and orphans and Monopoly,
and I was gracious enough to lend you my doll
with the head on a string you could pull
to make her talk, and you were thrilled
by the strange radio voices, pronouncing
them ghosts of lost space travellers.

Still now we twirl in and out of tune.
Your gift of a jumping jack, a promise I never kept.
This unfinished jigsaw puzzle.
The death of stretch monster,
his green skin bleeding,
other lost fairy tales.

Star Spangled

I'm eleven, my Dad is posted from Dublin to New York, we're on the move again. On our arrival in the new world, my mother reads the notice board saying, *welcome to the land of hope and freedom, the most beautiful country on earth*, and shakes her head. 'Let's go shopping.' As if that'll cure our immigrant nostalgia.

She takes me to Caldor World, a planet populated by unicorns, Barbie dolls and cavorting Care Bears. I stare out over a sea of pink and purple, huge tidal waves of rainbows ridden by hideous Hello Kitties threaten to submerge me and I feel sick. I wander up and down the aisles assaulted by fluorescent orange love hearts and pastel princesses imprisoned in glitter. I search in vain for even the tiniest hint of black as the questions from school violently clash in my head;

> 'What's it like to just eat potatoes?
> What's it like to have pigs in your kitchen?
> What's it like to live in the middle of a war,
> to have no electricity, to have never seen
> television, to shit in a hole in the ground?
> Did you leave because of the famine?
> Do you wear only green, do you believe
> in leprechauns?'

My mother claims they're just curious but I know for a fact that they're just stupid. I tell the girl beside me with the sparkly fingernails that my Dad doesn't bother with banks, he keeps his money at the end of a rainbow, and she says she thinks that's really neat. It makes me so tired I haven't the strength to tell her I'm joking, that I'm going colour blind from all their ignorance and that I fucking hate the United States of America, one nation under God, indivisible, and they can shove their liberty and justice up their arse.

Athletics

In my teens I develop a phobia of pink,
suffer searing migraines, nose bleeds.
I'm suspected of anorexia,
but in fact the only thing I do is eat.
I defeat all efforts to fatten me up,
remaining anaemic, forgetful, and ungrateful.

My mother insists sports are good for me,
makes me join hockey, football,
softball, basketball, anything that hints
at being a team player.

The coach says, 'What you lack in talent,
you make up for in aggression.'
Even if I've a funny accent,
an unpronounceable name,
I'm excellent at keeping score.

My mother says, 'Don't be so unforgiving,'
but she never asks what her crime is.
She's not any better at being American than me.

My Dad says, 'Isn't it wonderful we're moving on'
offering me champagne, and looking so surprised
when I slam the door shouting, 'Fuck you.'

Not Mugged

We've moved back to Dublin
and I'm in the bathroom.

My brother's face is a patchwork of purple,
his cheekbone has a greenish tinge,
and there is a streak of yellow
under one of his eyes,
like the yellow brick road
going in the wrong direction.

His bottom lip is split right open
and I dab at it with a tissue,
but the blood keeps seeping through the white.

One of his teeth is loose and I tell him
not to mess with it, but he can't help
running his tongue around it,
like a question that has no answer.

His beautiful blond hair is matted to his head,
and I discover that's blood too,
as I rinse the sponge under the cold water tap.

He's sitting on the edge of the bath,
and he doesn't even wince as I apply more Dettol.
'I have to disinfect it,' I explain apologetically,
but he just nods and says, 'you won't tell Mum.'

It's a statement, not a question, we both know
she'd never let him out the door again.

He's fourteen years old and he tells me how
he was walking past the flats
when he hears this voice shouting,
'hey young fella, what you looking at?
You fucking cunt.'

He hadn't even seen them
so how could he be looking at them?

Next thing he knows he's on the ground
and these three blokes, maybe seventeen
or eighteen years of age,
are kicking him repeatedly in the head.

He tells this story dead pan without the slightest
emotion as I wash the footprints from his face.

The only point at which his voice cracks
is when he says, 'and they never even took
my money, they never even took my fucking money.'

For a second his eyes fill with the pointlessness
of it all, but he blinks and it's gone, and I realise
nothing scares me more than his courage.

Immigrant

I graduate by doing what I always said I wouldn't,
emigrating to outer space, inner London. I say to my
mother, 'I've been very stupid.' She replies, 'Are you
pregnant?' I've never felt more empty. The city seems
to drain me of all sense of identity. We're crossing
Tottenham High Road when a woman yells at me,
'why don't you go back to your own country?'
I feel like telling her how much I wish I could.
In a pub in Seven Sisters, a man with a spider's web
tattooed on his face asks me if I'm a terrorist.
'Chucky ar la' he slurs and winks at me lecherously.
I can't help feeling my day will never come.

My boyfriend says he needs more space, more time,
more distance. He talks a lot about existentialism,
Simone De Beauvoir, and the need to be free from
bourgeois oppression and fidelity. This is why
he rarely comes home before midnight
if he comes home at all.

My lungs fill with loneliness as I struggle to breathe.
I've no idea what's wrong with me as time freezes
over but I seem to be fading. It's like looking
at myself through the wrong end of a telescope.

The boiler breaks again, but we've no money to fix it.
The doctor tells me I've chronic bronchitis; funny
it feels remarkably like homesickness or my trouble
with invisibility.

I take to crying in airports, taxi queues, train stations.
Then I find a job in TV and everyone tells me how
lucky I am. Suddenly we're the perfect couple, flat
in Chelsea, endless parties. I look in the mirror
but there's nobody there.

How can I be depressed if I don't exist?

Mutant

Next thing I'm shivering to death in a very long queue for a very trendy club. A boy wearing silver stars on a skin tight top shouts that if we're queer, we can skip to the front, if we're straight, we'll have to wait. Even though they're unlikely to test me on the door, I refuse to lie.

My honesty turns out to be somewhat ironic as once inside I knock back several more drinks and end up kissing a girl I've never met before. My friends think this is hilarious, as does my boyfriend, right up to the moment I announce I'm leaving him. Then he says he feels betrayed. My friends start to ask what this says about my sexuality and have I really considered whether this is a lifestyle choice I might regret? Meaning they have every intention of making me regret it as rooms fall silent when I enter them and I discover that same sex snogging for fun is fine, anyone can go through a phase or two, but being a fully fledged lesbian is not.

But for the first time I realize I really don't give a shit what anyone else thinks. Of course they'll be upset, what else are parents for, but they'll get over it. I rehearse my great speech that will scythe through their ignorance and prejudice. I'm a hero again, like when I was a kid, the words flowing through me an electric current. Like Wonder Woman, I've got truth on my side. And Batman and Robin made a perfectly good go of it, so why shouldn't I? Doubtless there'll be something of an explosion, kind of like a meteorite hitting the earth, but once the dust has settled, I'll still be their daughter, won't I?

Scared

The night before
my grand performance, my Dad
rings to tell me my mother's in the hospital,
some kind of tests, nothing to worry about,
his voice has the slightest tremor,
and suddenly I'm not in the story I thought I was,
I'm in another country all together.

My mother says, 'I used to worry
you were too gentle for this world
but see how wrong I was.' I wrap her
in my arms knowing I'm no kind of protection.

My Dad says, 'There's all sorts of
medical advances, treatments, chemical therapies.'
For the first time I understand he's scared,
maybe even more scared than me.

Rocket Science

I'm in my parents' kitchen in Dublin.
The day I teach my father how to scramble eggs,
my mother is lying upstairs in bed,

the cancer having devoured her appetite
so that we spend hours scouring
the supermarket shelves for food
pale enough not to make her puke.

I crack each egg so hard, it might as well be
my father's heart I'm breaking.
'Just a splash of milk,' I explain.

The look of intense concentration on his face
tells me he'll never manage it.
I grit my teeth and repeat, 'it's not rocket science.'

He replies, 'let me write this down,
how many eggs?' The pen
a pointless sword in his hand.

I try to make a joke of it to my mother
but she curls her sadness around the bitter
aftertaste of my voice.

'You have to understand,' she takes my hand in hers,
'if he learnt how to do it, it'd be like admitting
he's going to be on his own.'

I think then of how she's spent
the last quarter of a century
cooking his dinner,

and of all the things
they've been through together
that I'll never understand,

and what do I know about love
or rocket science anyway?

Truth

I tell my brother, 'I feel helpless.'
He says, 'I know, you've always
been a terrible liar.'

I never meant to weave myself
into such a strange place,
to hurt them by being so foreign,
so far, so heavy with secrets.

My mother says, 'Why can't people
just tell me the truth, I know
I'm dying, I'm not a child,
and neither are you.'

Damned if I do and damned if I don't,
I would give anything not to be this catch 22.
I say to my mother, 'I've something to tell you.'
She replies, 'Are you pregnant?'

Which is nearly funny,
but I've lost my sense of irony.

Afterwards my mother says, 'It crossed my mind,
I guessed there was something, I thought
maybe a married man or ...'

My Dad stares at me and whispers
after an eternity or two,
'Well it never crossed mine.'

I feel like a changeling, a cuckoo,
maybe the tags got mixed up in the hospital
and they took the wrong child home.

My mother says, 'Just make sure you enjoy your life.'
My Dad says, 'I'm on your side.'
which is courageous and kind.

I tell my brother, 'I'm in love with her.'
He says, 'I know, I always knew.'
and then we both laugh till we cry.

Stop

A young woman is sat in a car with her father.
They're stopped at some traffic lights.
Her father turns and stares at her.
He ignores the fact that the lights turn green.
He ignores the horns blaring behind him.

'How long do you think she's got?'
he asks his daughter as if she were the one deciding.

'Days. I think we're talking about days, Dad.'
Her father starts to tremble. His knuckles
are white from clutching the steering wheel.
'You really think she's going to die?'

She realizes then what her mother meant
when she said, 'I promised I'd never leave him,
he still thinks in spite of everything
that I never will.'

Love

My mother asks me to walk her to the hospice chapel.

It's just at the end of the corridor but we move
at a glacial pace. My mother leans on me,
she weighs nothing.

My Dad asks, 'have you noticed how she's
getting younger?' It's true; her eyes are
the deepest green, her skin translucent.

We sit and pray. 'Please God,' I think over
and over. I don't know what I believe any more,
I don't know what it is I'm asking for.

My mother says, 'funny how now I'm dying,
I've never felt so alive. After all, kiddo,
love is love. I've been very lucky really.'

Anne's Garden

It's a small white room.
There are flowers everywhere.
My mother adores the colours.
'Look at that peach. Isn't it amazing?'

I know it's partly the morphine,
but I feel I can see those colours blazing too,
as if blue has become more blue,
red has become more red,
a single shoot of green has become
the most precious extraordinary proof of life.

The doctor comes in so I go and sit
outside my mother's room to wait.
There is a painting on the wall, donated
by the family of someone who died here.
It's called *Anne's Garden*.

I wonder who Anne was and if she loved gardening
the way my mother does, the way my mother did.
I walk into the swirling flowers of the picture
as if they are the only thing that can save me
from this collapse of the present tense.

Blessing

I take my father on holidays to the west of Ireland. We've never been away together, just the two of us. Without my mother to translate, I don't know what we'll have to say to each other.

Everyone, from the hotel receptionist who winks at me as my Dad asks for two single rooms, to the waiter in the restaurant offering us roses, to the lady in the pub who asks how we met, assumes we're a couple. They're so unsubtle even my Dad notices. I'm terrified he'll be offended but he just says, 'well it's the first time in months anyone's looked at me with envy rather than pity.'

There's an old man in the corner of the pub playing the fiddle like it's about to catch fire and for a moment my Dad looks like he's enjoying himself.

Afterwards in the hotel bar, I attempt to ask him how he really is. He peers at me through his whiskey glass and says, 'It's all my fault. I'm the one that killed her.'

Having blamed my father all my life for so many things that really weren't his doing, I can't bear to watch him drowning in his own regrets. 'No, you didn't, Dad. You did everything you possibly could and she knew that.' 'But if we hadn't moved, if she hadn't got so stressed, if she'd gone to a doctor sooner...' My father's crying now. For possibly the first time since I was a small child, I take his hand. 'Dad, she loved you and she loved the life you had together. She would hate you to torture yourself like this.'

My father smiles at me. 'You're very like her you know. I hope you'll find someone, it doesn't really matter who they are, that appreciates how kind you are.'

It hits me how much I've always needed his blessing.

The Red Phone

I think of her sometimes in the long afternoons
as the last of the light plays on the windows.
Two small boys pass below on their bikes,
one of them – his face split with a grin – look, no hands!
racing down hill at top speed, not a care in the world.
What happens to that recklessness?

When I was a small child, one of the many winters
I got sick in my chest, each breath a small incision,
my mother set up these toy red telephones
with a white cord that ran all the way from my bedroom
down the stairs and into the kitchen.

Anything I wanted, tea, cookies, more steam,
all I'd to do is pick up that red phone
which connected only to her.
Her voice crackling down the line,
her footstep on the stair,
and me nestled into the covers
like a small mouse in its nest,
a tiny fragment of a world.

When she died, I thought of all the times
she'd rung me at work, or when
I was hurrying out the door to the pub,
and how quick and casual I'd been,

answering her questions of concern
with that same shortness of breath,
trying to get her off the line
with the minimum of explanations,
as if danger were just another one of her myths
and I had grown up as invincible as her.

Now in the quiet of these January afternoons,
when my lungs are weighed down with snow
and everything seems so uncertain,
I can't help wishing I'd somehow
kept that red telephone.

Epilogue

I'm out there in space,
floating through my own radio waves,
unable to get a signal, when you say
the taxi is taking far too long

so I follow your orbit through streets stripped bare
of their shadows. It seems I'll have to reach across
light years to touch you, as if I've embedded myself
in some invisible force of gravity.

Burning through the uncertainties of black holes,
where what goes up may not come down,
I feel like the after dust of a shooting star,

the light that still travels even though the centre
is gone, the glowing ash of that last cigarette
when you know this time you really have quit.

I'm sitting in the silence of my rocket ship,
the final engine having given up the ghost,
my days suspended in waiting.

Sputnik countdowns repeating endlessly in my head.
What will happen when I hit the atmosphere of your kiss?
It's been years since I lost touch with ground control.

I can't say I care much for time travel, the late night
chill of empty platforms, the cancellation of schedules,
my suitcase getting heavier.

I bet I've forgotten my toothbrush,
along with supernovas, and the reason I wanted
to be an astronaut in the first place.

You tell me it's not far now. Light and warmth
and the startling smallness of our bodies
curled in moon shapes. As if the names of planets

have been wiped clean and I can leap
across desert oceans, no spacesuit needed,
as I finally figure out that it might be safe to land.

Aoife Mannix is an Irish writer & poet based in London. In addition to regular performances throughout the UK, she has performed her poetry in Taiwan, Thailand, India, Norway and Austria with the British Council. She has previously toured as part of *accents on words* (tall lighthouse), *Writers on the Storm* (Apples & Snakes) & *Kin* (Renaissance One). Her work has been widely published in magazines and anthologies as well as being broadcast on BBC Radio. Her first full collection of poetry *the elephant in the corner* was published by tall lighthouse in 2005.

Janie Armour is a composer, musical director & accordionist. She has over 30 professional theatre shows to her credit, including composition for the Watermill Theatre, Newbury & 12 shows for Chichester Festival Theatre. She has performed as the accordionist in *Piaf* (York Theatre Royal) & in *The Life of Galileo* (Royal National Theatre). As well as accordion, Janie plays piano and mandolin & has performed with bands & poets at festivals throughout the UK & Europe, including Lisbon International Festival, WOMAD, Glastonbury, Leeds International, Munich Festival, Golowan Festival in Penzance & Vlissingen Street Festival, Holland.

Kerry Bradley - this is Kerry's second design for Apples & Snakes, after designing *Broken Words* in 2005. Kerry works as a Theatre Designer & Lecturer, as well as a Production Buyer & Set Dresser in Television & Film. She has designed many new (and old) plays in London, on tour & in regional repertory theatres including Leicester Haymarket and the Palace Theatre, Westcliff. Recent designs include *Heroes* for the National Theatre & *Romeo and Juliet* for The Lord Chamberlain's Men. Production Buyer & Set dresser credits include *Jim Jam and Sunny*, *Dolphins* and *Footballer's Wives*. Kerry currently teaches on the Design for Stage and Screen course at Wimbledon School of Art.

Mike Kirchner is a freelance producer & director who began life as a performer with the extraordinary Talking Birds. He devised & toured with them until 1998 & subsequently with Birmingham's finest international export, theatre makers Stan's Cafe. Since 2004 Mike has worked with Apples & Snakes to assist, produce & direct varied artists, each with their own unique take on the future of spoken word. Collaborations have included co-producing Lemn Sissay's successful UK & international performances of Something Dark & co-directing Zena Edwards whose new work Security will tour from 2008.